PRINCIPLES FOR CAPITAL ALLOCATION IN BUSINESS SECURITIES AND OTHER WRITINGS

GUILLERMO ESTEFANI MONÁRREZ

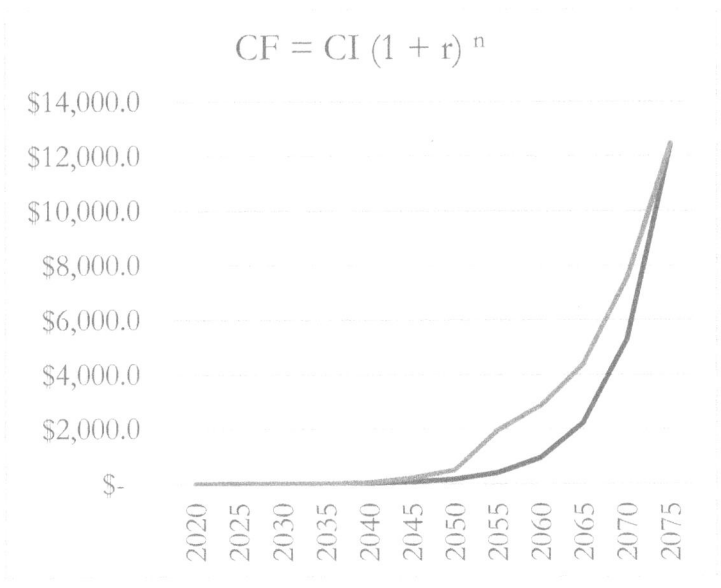

Index

Foreword 5
Introduction 9
1   Principles of purpose 15
    1.1   Principle of value 17
    1.2   Principle of character 27
    1.3   Principle of entropy 35
    1.4   Principle of problems 45
    1.5   Principle of the future 53
    1.6   Principle of capital 57
    1.7   Principle of businesses 65
2   Principles of form 69
    2.1   Principle of analysis 71
    2.2   Principle of the macroeconomic 77
    2.3   Principle of money inflation 83
    2.4   Principle of credit interest 89
    2.5   Principle of taxes for the public interest 93
    2.6   Principle of the financial system 97
    2.7   Principle of international trade 103
    2.8   Principle of industry 105
    2.9   Principle of seeking opportunities 109
    2.10 Principle of business securities 113
    2.11 Principle of stewardship 115

2.12 Principle of creativity 123
2.13 Principle of distribution 127
3 Principles of act 131
   3.1 Principle of investment 133
   3.2 Principle of the investment approach 137
   3.3 Principle of the market 141
   3.4 Principle of the investment moment 151
   3.5 Principle of the margin of safety 155
   3.6 Principle of capital allocation 159
4 Appendix 165
5 Bibliographic references 172
6   Personal thanks 174
7 About the author 177

Foreword

When we mention the word "finance," we often think of complex equations and specialized interpretations. Similarly, capital allocation is often associated with buying and selling stocks for profit, with images of Wall Street traders and brokers analyzing charts and news, attempting to time their trades for maximum gains.

However, the process of capital allocation goes beyond these surface-level perceptions. It requires investors to have a genuine interest in the well-being of society and a vision for a better future.

Furthermore, it necessitates a thorough analysis of the businesses where capital will be invested, assessing their potential for growth and stability within a macroeconomic context.

In this concise yet significant book, Estefani synthesizes the contributions of prominent investment theorists, presenting their principles in a clear and profound manner.

The text explains concepts that may initially appear dense but gradually intertwines them to reveal their essential meaning. The ultimate result is a set of criteria that any investor would benefit from considering before making capital allocation decisions. Adhering to these principles can contribute to the survival and growth of businesses that generate social value while discouraging those that may have detrimental effects.

From my perspective, the collective contribution of these principles lies in investing in businesses that strive to create a better world. This means selecting instruments that represent companies capable of pursuing the greater good through innovative and sustainable solutions.

Estefani emphasizes the importance of establishing relationships based on quality, trust, and responsibility. Although he doesn't explicitly state it, he implicitly raises the following questions: To whom would you entrust your money for growth? Would you leave the future of your children in just anyone's hands? When we allocate capital, we are essentially entrusting the responsibility for society's future. Let us do so wisely.

I won't delve further into the subject; instead, I encourage you to read this fascinating document. I can attest to Estefani's passion for finance and knowledge, but more importantly, he is a person worthy of trust. So, enjoy his work.

Dr. Hugo Briseño Ramírez

January 30, 2020

Introduction

The best way to start anything is from its fundamental principles. Benjamin Graham once said, "Sound results come from using sound principles."

First and foremost, I want to express my gratitude for taking the time to explore this work.

As the title suggests, this book presents essential principles that can help you transform cash into capital and allocate it to business ventures that contribute to a more prosperous future.

At the beginning, you might find the work conceptually dense and philosophical. I encourage you to continue reading, despite the initial complexity or any perceived disconnection from the central topic.

As you progress through the pages, you will notice that the concepts gradually come together, forming a cohesive structure. Each person may find different parts of the book more enjoyable, depending on their temperament.

While I dedicate a section to reviewing well-known concepts related to the stock market, these principles can also be applied to capital allocation in non-publicly traded companies.

Please note that this is not a motivational or personal finance book. It does not delve into the analysis and operation of preferred stocks, corporate debt, government bonds, initial public offerings, or specialized opportunities such as arbitrage, bankruptcies, mergers, divestitures, and acquisitions.

Although many of these principles can be useful in various investment and business fields, the book does not focus on economic values tied to durable goods like precious metals or real estate. Furthermore, it does not provide shortcuts or formulas for complex assets such as futures contracts, currencies, or cryptocurrencies encrypted in blockchains. Each of these domains requires specific knowledge and principles of its own.

Just because this book is concise and uses simple language does not mean it lacks substance or that the topics discussed are of little importance. On the contrary, the intention is to distill the concepts to provide greater density rather than volume, enabling you to learn in a relatively short time and in an enjoyable manner. By the end, you will have a comprehensive and clear understanding of this discipline.

Due to its concentrated nature, this book may help you discover concepts through your own personal experiences or by revisiting the text at a later time. I acknowledge the lack of didactic examples or demonstrations intentionally, as I prioritize consistency.

I understand that gathering resources for a purpose can be challenging, and the task of capital allocation can be exhausting and even painful if not approached with care.

While some individuals may learn through trial and error, following the willful mindset of Thomas Alva Edison, it is important to recognize that there is a lack of investment culture in Latin America, especially outside privileged circles. Starting without a clear idea can be confusing for many, and limited resources may unfortunately lead to significant losses. As Nikola Tesla once said, "With a little theory and calculation, you can save up to ninety percent of the work."

Based on my experience, I know that there is a scarcity of reliable and didactic materials, alongside an overwhelming number of opinions that emerge daily regarding the "correct" way to engage in this activity. These opinions may come from financial product sellers, bankers, entrepreneurs, employees, journalists, public servants, consultants, and finance experts. While most of these individuals are intelligent, it is important to acknowledge that they may not share the same intentions, risk profiles, or goals as we do.

For a third of my life, I have dedicated myself to gathering, understanding, and applying these principles taught by exceptional teachers, even though I have not had the privilege of meeting them in person due to constraints of time, distance, and opportunity. I am fully aware that my journey as an investor is still to be written over the coming decades, if I am fortunate enough to have a long life. However, this does not prevent me from examining these principles, much like a physicist studying the universe to contribute to an interstellar exploration mission.

Therefore, I ask you to consider this work as a serious opinion from an admirer of the most generous teachers in this discipline. Many of the ideas presented here can be further explored through the bibliographic references provided at the end.

As time passes, I hope to refine my use of these principles and continue to develop and mature them. Although it is a modest contribution, my sincere desire is for this book to bring something positive into your life, propelling us further as a civilization and ensuring a brighter future for all humanity.

Lastly, if you were to ask me in an elevator what successful capital allocation activity entails, I would tell you that it is akin to building lasting friendships. Personally, I will always choose to invest my resources, time, intellect, and energy in understanding the genuine passion of those who strive daily to create value, rather than succumbing to the ordinary deceptions of those who prefer ambiguity, confusion, and lack of clarity.

Guillermo Estefani Monárrez
January 2020

1 Principles of purpose

Reasons and motives for capital allocation

1.1 Principle of value

The principle of value creation lies in consciousness.

Through consciousness, we perceive our existence and recognize the external world as reality.

It enables us to engage in intimate self-reflection, absorb information, pay attention, remain vigilant, reason, make judgments, decisions, interact with others, take action, and be accountable for our choices.

Consciousness allows us to acknowledge that everything in the cosmos serves a purpose. This can be observed in language, life itself, the intricate nature of human consciousness, the form and organization of perceivable objects, and the discoveries made through scientific advancements.

The concept of "system" emerged relatively recently, during the 19th century, as humanity began developing industrial machines with the aid of thermodynamics' findings.

When we think about systems, we simply aim to identify their constituent elements and understand the correlations through which these elements interact to form a whole.

To describe systems, we establish definitions, purposes, concepts, organizational logics, and boundaries that determine which elements belong to a system within model and which ones exist in the surrounding environment, with which the system interacts as part of a larger domain.

Consciousness empowers us to comprehend both the simplest and most complex systems. It enables us to observe, quantify existing phenomena, and recall past events.

Through reason, we can grasp the principles governing mathematical abstractions and use them to create models for the future. Additionally, consciousness grants us the capacity for compassion, empathy, or even animosity towards our fellow beings.

Consciousness is in a constant state of change as we learn and interact with others. It allows us to establish priorities and value systems or principles that guide our actions as we progress through life, striving to achieve objectives, ideals, and rewards.

Consciousness enables us to set goals and purposes. As human beings, our general aspiration is to live a fruitful life. Many of us seek a life of learning, hoping to minimize inconveniences and stumbles. However, when challenges do arise, we aim to face them with the utmost emotional, spiritual, and physical satisfaction.

This desire is to live in "the good." As Marcus Aurelius Antoninus (121-180 AD) emphasized, "Everything is in our minds; that is, despite the existence of an objective 'good' in life, a significant portion of our experiences depends on how we perceive and appreciate the life we lead."

Subjectively, "the good" can be described as a present state of dignity and inner harmony, where satisfaction, joy, and gratitude prevail in our experiences.

We yearn to embrace life passionately and continue living. We want reality to be perceived as an enduring and multiplying phenomenon, not fleeting, and we envision the future as a situation that holds the promise of improvement, despite present adversities.

Although it may seem like an ideal, we long for the tangible certainty of "the good" in our daily lives. We desire "the good" to be real and consistent, not merely a concept or proclamation from others.

The longing for "the good" stands in contrast to the natural tendency of the material universe towards chaos and decay, which represents randomness and disorder.

Acting intelligently in pursuit of the "good," counteracting disorder, lies at the heart of "value." Acting with value yields confidence and dispels the uncertainty of falsehood.

Through consciousness, we reason, question the state of things, seek resources to fulfill our needs, express art, communicate, develop technology, embrace our sexuality, establish social structures, nurture culture, venerate the divine, and direct our energies towards loftier goals. In essence, consciousness allows us to continually shape our environment.

Although our bodies are vulnerable to the wild state of nature, we possess consciousness that enables us to cooperate in complex communities and tame the wilderness.

This process involves understanding how nature operates, the resources available to us, and utilizing them to create technology that improves our material living conditions. Consequently, we have intentionally adapted to nearly any environment on Earth, according to our perception of what is "good."

Determining what constitutes "good" is influenced by subjective factors. For instance, our language, spiritual beliefs, social or family status, self-image, profession, leisure interests, personal preferences, and our valuation of material wealth.

There are also environmental factors that shape our perception of "good," such as climate, weather, the state of the economy (whether society is experiencing depression and scarcity or prosperity with abundant resources), living in times of peace or war, and the availability and accessibility of health, education, and transportation services.

Intimate factors, like our personality, health, friendships, acts of generosity, the cultivation of virtues or vices (e.g., exercise or substance use), and our definitions of attitudes like modesty, humility, or arrogance, also impact our perception of "good."

Recognizing this, we understand that human life is inherently diverse, and we coexist within various domains or fields, including politics, sports, art, academia, family, professions, and business. Consequently, each domain is governed by values, which may or may not intersect or conflict with one another.

This perspective also allows us to differentiate between two major aspects when assessing the value of something: objective value and subjective value. However, due to the nature of judgments, it is challenging to clearly distinguish one from the other.

Objective value refers to the value of actions or objects under examination. It encompasses specific attributes such as the work performed, the magnitude of change achieved, complexity, order, and the intentional modification of reality.

Consider the sun as an example of intrinsic value. It undergoes changes, performs work, and releases energy, which is captured by ocean plankton, transforming it into chemical energy. This energy sustains life by serving as food for larger sea creatures and facilitating oxygen production on Earth. This process occurs without human intervention.

Now, let's think about cereal seeds. Humans have domesticated them over millennia, selectively choosing those with greater productivity. We sow and harvest them, but they cannot be easily digested until we grind them into flour.

With flour and water, we can create yeast cultures, which, through the yeast's fermentation and the dough's exposure to heat, transform these seeds into bread.

In this case, human hands did not invent the seeds, yeast, or fire; they merely guided nature under a specific order to produce something beneficial for life. This exemplifies intrinsic value, irrespective of individual preferences for bread.

Another way to grasp intrinsic value is to consider that, regardless of others' opinions, we would likely prefer to see ourselves as courageous and valuable rather than cowardly and helpless.

While examples abound, these three illustrate the concept of intrinsic value effectively.

However, it's important to recognize that the valuation of something always involves an element of subjective reasoning, which can be prone to errors in appreciation, language's symbolic nature in describing ideas, and potential divergence from the actual reality.

Nonetheless, in practice, we can observe certain actions in others that we deem "brave," "intelligent," or performed "with passion." Although accurately measuring the intensity of these qualities is challenging, we can still distinguish and contrast such acts with those we consider "cowardly" or wasteful.

Extrinsic value, or subjective value, is precisely the personal assessment we make regarding the value of things. It arises from the esteem, honor, and collective agreement within our community regarding certain actions or objects.

Since value represents actions that are beneficial for life, we strive to cultivate values in all aspects and fields of our lives, including economic values.

However, we mustn't forget that the most precious pursuit in our quest for values is the development of our consciousness, as it lies at the core of our humanity.

Therefore, nurturing and expanding our consciousness should be our utmost priority, demanding our attention and efforts.

1.2 Principle of character

Many of these recommendations have been proposed and practiced since ancient times, forming the foundation of human civilization. They are presented here not as a personal burden or a tool to judge others, but as a framework or guide to enhance our effectiveness in carrying out our tasks.

It's important to clarify that not having this list of desires doesn't mean we're forbidden from engaging in capital allocation activities. However, following these suggestions can undoubtedly lead to better results. Our character defines how our conscience thinks and acts, setting us apart from others.

According to Benjamin Graham, developing good character is more crucial for success in investment activities than having a brilliant mind. In my view, the term "courageous character" aptly describes what we mean by a "good character" (brave or valuable character also work well!).

Equipping ourselves with a courageous character allows us to face adversity with the belief that we can emerge stronger from it.

Philip Fisher identifies three demonstrations of character that can ensure success in any aspect of life: "Success = 2i + 1h." These demonstrations are integrity, ingenuity, and hard work.

When a young shareholder of Berkshire Hathaway asked Charlie Munger for advice on achieving success in life, his response was straightforward: "Don't do cocaine. Don't race trains to the track. And avoid all AIDS situations."

Although this may sound amusing, it's much more complex in everyday life. To achieve success, we must avoid making mistakes. The corollary is simple: Instead of doubling our efforts to recover from a mistake, if we double our efforts without making that mistake in the first place, we will go much further.

Now, I believe that the foundation for developing a courageous character lies in "humility." The term "humility" etymologically relates to "having our feet on the ground." Paradoxically, "humility" shares the same root as "humanity" and "humor".

What I want to emphasize is that humility involves recognizing our status as living beings made of dust, susceptible to error and deception.

It means accepting that we can make mistakes and acknowledging our imperfections, rather than behaving with pride or arrogance.

Humility enables us to acknowledge our scope and limitations and admit our mistakes. Through humility, we can work on improving all the other aspects of our character.

By embracing our ignorance, we cease believing that we are smarter than others who share society with us, and we offer them respect instead. Moreover, we overcome the folly of assuming things that are not reality and cease pretending to predict the future.

Humility helps us lead lives that align our thoughts and words, allowing our minds to perceive clearly and discern deception and lies, which are the sources of prejudice. It also enables us to communicate openly, clearly, and directly with our peers in all matters.

Being humble enables us to exercise caution and moderation, considering both opportunities and risks, as well as recognizing the consequences of our actions. Humility allows us to accurately assess our own importance and acknowledge that our opinions may not always align closely with reality.

Humility is essential for respectfully acknowledging all kinds of mistakes, both our own and those of others. By achieving this, we can correct past mistakes and avoid making them in the future.

According to Warren Buffett, the most crucial errors in capital allocation are "errors of omission."

These mistakes, which are acts we did not commit, are difficult to recognize and admit. Victimizing ourselves, being self-indulgent, and justifying our actions hinder the development of humility.

Another fundamental trait required for this endeavor is "curiosity." It involves using our intellect but also relies on intuition and instincts.

Through curiosity, we discern the good and valuable and understand their degrees of intensity. It expands our language skills, allowing us to better describe our thoughts, emotions, desires, intentions, and situations, thus guiding our actions more effectively.

Curiosity helps us comprehend risks, opportunities, limitations, and the scope of our resources. It enables us to question generalized opinions and compare them with our perception of reality, fostering "free thinking" and liberating us from mental traps.

Constantly driven by curiosity, we escape ignorance through learning. It demands disciplined reasoning and the pursuit of knowledge previously unknown to us.

Our intellect allows us to learn, process, distinguish, and classify information, leading to the formation of ideas.

It empowers us to devise algorithms—processes for organizing resources to achieve results.

Through curiosity, we discover complex interrelationships between algorithms and patterns, enhancing our problem-solving abilities and improving our lives.

Finally, to sustain the development of these traits, we need "perseverance." It requires faith, hope, and discipline to pursue our goals, even when others disagree.

Investment discipline is not a miraculous or shortcut approach but one that demands hard work and practicality.

Perseverance necessitates "patience" during challenging times. Accompanied by intellectual, spiritual, and material preparation, it helps us navigate market fluctuations.

While "capital" and "the market" are inherently complex, our greatest adversary is always ourselves. Therefore, it is crucial to cultivate the right thoughts, intellectual framework, mental attitudes, and temperament to make informed decisions and face adversity.

Let's acknowledge our limitations and be grateful for our current situation, finding satisfaction in how we've conducted our lives thus far.

This self-awareness allows us to have control over our senses, emotions, expectations, and actions.

As Benjamin Graham stated, we can only control our thoughts. This principle of character is essential for proper capital allocation.

Develop a courageous character, exemplified by integrity, ingenuity, and hard work. Avoid failures and cultivate humility, curiosity, and perseverance.

By embodying these traits, we gain valuable tools to network and engage in meaningful conversations with like-minded individuals interested in business and problem-solving.

Moreover, these traits serve as the foundation for developing the intrinsic value of our personal brand.

The more responsibility, respect, and seriousness we invest in this development, the greater the trust and dignity we will earn from others.

1.3 Principle of entropy

In the physical universe as we know it, there are three distinguishable elements: space, matter, and energy.

Everything in the universe, to our knowledge, is composed of matter and energy, which take various forms and combinations. Even atoms, the building blocks of matter, are not completely static due to the exchange of energy caused by gravity and electromagnetic forces.

While humans understand that the physical world exists independently of us, we strive to find coherence for our minds by identifying general patterns that describe the behavior of what exists. These patterns, which we call laws or principles, exhibit remarkable elegance and precision in explaining phenomena throughout the universe.

Albert Einstein's theory of general relativity is an example of such a law. However, exceptions may arise that require further calibration and experimentation as our technological advancements expand our knowledge.

We define "matter" as anything that occupies space and exists in different states in the universe.

Through astrophysics, we have observed the behavior of hydrogen and helium atoms as they agglomerate under high temperatures and pressures, forming stars like the Sun.

These stars act as thermonuclear engines, with atoms existing in a plasma state, subjected to the immense pressure resulting from the interplay of gravity and electromagnetic forces.

This process generates energy, such as gamma rays, which travel through space, reaching our planet after passing through our magnetosphere. This energy nourishes our flora and the plankton in our oceans, significantly influencing our climate.

Furthermore, we continuously theorize and experiment with nature, seeking to understand what would occur if matter were to approach absolute zero and exploring situations relevant to human life.

Regarding matter, we have learned that the mass of a body depends on the density of protons and neutrons within its atoms, multiplied by the number of atoms comprising it.

In the late 17th century, Isaac Newton discovered that material bodies possess an inherent tendency to attract one another, altering their trajectories based on the distances between them.

This attraction is influenced by a universal gravitational constant (g). When bodies draw closer to each other, the acceleration of attraction intensifies.

This principle of mechanics provided accurate calculations for the initial stages of space exploration.

However, at the beginning of the 20th century, Albert Einstein theorized that gravity is, in fact, a geometric deformation of space and time, primarily occurring around a body.

This groundbreaking concept aided our comprehension of phenomena such as "black holes," whose intrinsic nature remains a mystery today.

Energy, on the other hand, is considered the capacity to act, operate, or perform work on matter, rather than an intangible substance. We view energy as the cause of events, and it can be either "potential" or "actual."

Our understanding of "light," encompassing all forms of radiation in the universe, including what we perceive with our eyes, has also improved. This radiation charges, energizes, and propels matter, leading to movement and changes in states.

Through calculations, humans have determined the finite and constant speed at which light travels through empty space. According to Albert Einstein's Theory of General Relativity, no material object can surpass this universal constant known as the speed of light (c), which is approximately 299,792 kilometers per second (186,282 miles per second!). Information cannot be transmitted faster than this speed either.

Einstein also elucidated how energy is transported, transformed, and encapsulated in an equation that governs the universe, rather than being something that can be destroyed.

As a result, we have formulated the "First Law of Thermodynamics," which states that if we were to sum up all the energy and mass in the universe, the total would always remain constant.

Considering the First Law of Thermodynamics, which asserts that energy cannot be created or destroyed but merely transformed, we can understand that whenever a change or transformation occurs in reality, the energy transferred will never be entirely utilized. Some energy will be "wasted" in the form of heat.

This dissipation of energy as heat not only produces change but also introduces disorder into the state of things. Consequently, the overall system tends toward a more chaotic configuration than the previous state.

By capturing photographs that depict the changing system, reflecting its tendency to disorder, we can perceive the rate at which these changes occur. This measurement is known as entropy.

As the system becomes more disordered, the entropy increases, indicating a shift towards randomness and maximum disorder, which we interpret as a state of equilibrium. The "Second Law of

Thermodynamics" informs us that entropy in the universe tends to increase.

Thanks to humility, we can recognize that most things in the universe exist independently of human intervention. Humans did not create light, matter, black holes, galaxies, stars, or the hydrogen clouds that form celestial bodies.

These bodies are constantly changing, contributing to the increasing entropy in our cosmos.

Therefore, by simply existing, we inadvertently modify reality, resulting in the inevitable waste of energy and the continuous increase of disorder in the universe.

This understanding helps us grasp the concept of time, which allows us to comprehend the orderly progression of things. Time enables us to perceive the existence of objects and their dynamics of transformation in space.

For instance, what we directly experience is "the present." We acknowledge that it arises from an irreversible previous state, which we call "the past." We also understand that the current situation will transition into an unpredictable future. Time, for us humans, is the essence of life, and we measure its passage through the events that occur.

As the universe undergoes constant change, we perceive that life continues relentlessly, irrespective of our personal circumstances.

However, this perception influences our understanding of the passage of time. As the song "Il Mondo" performed by Jimmy Fontana poetically expresses[1]:

> "The world spins in endless space, even if love is born or ends, even if there is joy and pain of people like me.
>
> Oh world! Now I look at you, I lose myself in your silence, and I am nothing by your side.
>
> The world never stopped for a single moment, the night always follows the day, and the day will continue."

---

[1] Lyrics from "IL Mondo" of 1965 © Universal Music Publishing Group, song composed by Gianni Meccia, Carlos Pes, Lilli Greco and Jimmy Fontana with arrangement of Ennio Morricone.

Returning to the physical aspect of time, if space is continuous, then time is also continuous, as there is no definitive way to measure its passage.

Additionally, Newton's "First Law of Inertia" states that an object at rest will remain unchanged until acted upon by an external force.

Thus, when humans measure time, we are essentially measuring the movement of objects. We rely on clocks, significant historical moments, or the celestial bodies' travel as references to quantify the passage of time.

From this, we deduce that time exists only in the presence of change. Moreover, entropy allows us to logically explain the significance of events.

A practical example of observing the effect of entropy in our daily lives is the wisdom passed down by our grandparents when our new shoes would wear out, teaching us that "everything wears out with use."

Warren Buffett also acknowledges this effect in business, emphasizing that growth cannot be limitless because "trees do not grow to the sky."

Although this phenomenon has been observed throughout history, formal discussions regarding it began with David Ricardo in the early 19th century, and it is now associated with entropy. The "Law of Diminishing Returns" applies to nearly all aspects of nature.

In simple terms, this principle states that the growth of a productive system has limits, and as it develops, subsequent changes become progressively smaller.

It applies to new items that deteriorate with use, as well as to the diminishing satisfaction we experience when taking subsequent bites of a delicious meal.

Another perspective on this principle is that seizing an opportunity diminishes its potential. Throughout human existence, we have sought to explain these phenomena to ensure the progress of our lives.

Since these phenomena are inherent in nature and transcend our opinions, ignoring them does not exempt us from experiencing their implications. Deliberately disregarding them can lead to errors.

We must also acknowledge that the business world is infinitesimally small compared to the vast domain of existence. It is not exempt from the passage of time or the influence of entropy.

Therefore, it is crucial to consider these principles in the business world, tempering the excitement that accompanies any entrepreneurial endeavor.

1.4 Principle of problems

A problem is an obstacle, difficulty, or question that hinders the achievement of our goals or desires. When faced with a problem, we experience restlessness and seek to eliminate it.

Sometimes problems seem incomprehensible, falling into the realm of the impossible or the mysterious. In such cases, we learn to coexist with their presence. However, when problems are well-defined, we search for general approaches to solve them and develop specific plans accordingly. Unfortunately, our understanding of problems is often influenced by unintentional mental constructs known as "cognitive biases." These biases limit our ability to perceive things accurately.

For instance, we tend to seek information that aligns with our pre-existing ideas. We also have a tendency to solve new problems using previously successful solutions, resisting the exploration of different approaches.

There are instances when we insist on using familiar tools in the way we were taught. When we come together as a group to solve a problem, we often converge on a single perspective, which can limit our range of solutions.

Furthermore, we sometimes mistake collecting irrelevant information for gaining a deeper understanding of the problem, unintentionally making it more complex. We may become fixated on certain aspects of the problem out of curiosity or ego, losing sight of the essential elements we need to address. As a result, our problem-solving efforts become ineffective.

Overcoming these obstacles is challenging if we embrace ignorance, fear, or rush to judge without sufficient evidence. However, with a cultivated character, the task becomes easier.

Solving problems requires the use of our intellect. We must interpret the situation and its context, apply relevant rules, and keep the ultimate goal in mind to find optimal solutions.

A problem becomes truly human when it affects at least one conscious being. For example, an earthquake does not constitute a human problem unless someone is at risk of suffering from its consequences. An earthquake of significant magnitude on the planet Jupiter, for instance, is not yet a human problem.

Social problems arise when at least two conscious beings are invested in a particular issue, resulting in controversy due to differing positions on its resolution.

As human beings, we yearn to live. We have needs, desires, and, as Viktor Frankl observed, the "choice of our personal attitude towards circumstances." With physical and moral freedom, we can decide how we treat others and how we utilize the time and resources at our disposal.

We are not born in isolation but as part of a community. At birth, the first social connections are formed, creating familial and emotional bonds.

This gives rise to an unspoken yet understood solidarity, a collective desire for life to endure and transcend despite the challenges of entropy. Thus, we witness the origin of human problems.

As life progresses, we encounter a multitude of problems. If we were to describe all these problems, along with the ideas implemented to solve them, for every individual who has ever existed, we would gain insight into the composition of human civilization.

Our understanding is limited, but our desire to live knows no bounds, while our resources are subject to entropy. This magnifies the magnitude of humanity's problems.

Throughout history, we have relied on our collective consciousness to organize ourselves into societies, specialize in various disciplines, establish rules of coexistence, and institute authorities, among other endeavors.

In a sense, we have developed a social algorithm that influences our decision-making processes, including consumption and production.

Given that everyone wants to live, our focus inevitably turns towards the resources and vital spaces we perceive as available.

This leads to competition and the emergence of countless social problems and power dynamics. Resolving these problems involves law, authority, force, crime, social interactions, agreements, and commerce.

Power is the capacity to alter reality and is inherent in all living beings. Similar to energy, which enables work to be done on matter, power can be observed as either "potential" or "actual," indicating its ubiquity and its influence on our lives.

Michel Foucault refers to this aspect when he describes power as "something strategic." Humans intentionally and purposefully wield power to propel their lives forward.

A power relationship is built upon trust, forming a contract. Its essence lies in the ability to take action and make things happen in order to fulfill a promise, with the ultimate goal of advancing life.

When faced with a problem, a decision to exercise or refrain from using power becomes necessary.

Since power stems from the will to live, we can perceive it in all human relationships. Power can intertwine and become more intricate, giving rise to hierarchical structures based on contractual agreements. As a result, a group of people can achieve more collectively than an individual alone. At its highest level, this manifests as "government power" or "structural power," which operates within a given context and, with sufficient scale, can "organize and direct scenarios," as described by Eric R. Wolf, or in other words, "influence actions," according to Foucault.

It is important to remember that every human action generates entropy.

The consequence of acting to sustain life produces energy waste in the form of heat, resulting in disorder. Consequently, the aggregation of power structures for living also generates new realities, additional disorder, and thus, new problems.

Furthermore, power hierarchies are dynamic systems in constant flux. On one hand, those who govern within the power structure pursue "the good" for themselves and those they govern.

On the other hand, the structures themselves undergo degradation due to entropy, leading to imbalances and power struggles among those in power, those vying for power, and those governed by the structure.

In essence, the passage of time entails the creation and dismantling of power structures, accompanied by problems.

All these factors contribute to the reality that, in an entropic world, simply organizing ourselves collaboratively to overcome challenges and achieve "the good" for ourselves, our loved ones, and our peers is insufficient in resolving the rate at which new problems emerge.

Many individuals mistakenly believe that economic wealth holds the key to solving their problems, even if these issues stem from non-economic aspects of life. This is problematic.

One way to attain economic wealth is by systematically and consistently addressing problems in various areas of people's lives. Some individuals derive satisfaction from solving such problems. However, this situation impacts the nature of human relationships and generates further problems. This, too, poses a challenge.

1.5 Principle of the future

In Western cultures, humans perceive time as a linear path where the future represents the yet-to-occur portion. Using the information we believe we know, gathered from the past and our present sensory experiences, we attempt to speculate, project, calculate, and anticipate the forthcoming changes in order to create a forecast or model of the future.

If changes happen in a relatively consistent manner, and if we can fully identify the variables that determine their intensity and direction, our ability to predict their behavior improves.

A better understanding of the rate of change, the system being modeled, its current dynamics, and even its essence allows us to calibrate our future model more accurately.

This forms the foundation for developing future formulas, assuming the other variables remain unchanged.

However, since complete comprehension of all factors and the true nature of existence remains elusive, there will always be a risk or uncertainty that our models or speculations about the future might prove incorrect.

Therefore, our knowledge of future reality is imprecise or limited due to the possibility of unforeseen events or variables that were not properly considered.

It's important to acknowledge the significant role played by our animal instincts, intuition, emotions, prejudices, and value systems in shaping our worldview, information processing, and decision-making.

These factors hinder our ability to discern what is "real" from ambiguous imagination or speculation.

They limit our behavior and make us vulnerable to unintended consequences, resulting in loss or harm to ourselves or others.

This increases the likelihood of acting erroneously, relying on incomplete and generalized elements of what we perceive as reality.

When our consciousness engages in logical and sequential conjectures to describe the change in state or location in space and time that has yet to occur, we are contemplating the "future." Just as we describe the past as "irreversible" due to the direction of entropy, we can also assert that the future is "inevitable."

The future is something that will emerge from today. As time represents a rate of change, the future will differ from the present and will be shaped by the progress of life combined with the advancement of entropy in the universe. This renders the future "unpredictable."

Regarding entropy in the universe, as far as we know, its course cannot be halted.

However, when it comes to the progress of life, humans utilize technology to harness the resources of our environment according to our capabilities.

We have demonstrated this ability since ancient times when we created gardens, and it continues with the development of Artificial Intelligence technologies.

Hence, while we acknowledge the universe's eventual degradation since the dawn of time, we also possess the potential to anticipate positive outcomes to advance life. Consequently, we can act on a grand scale to make the world a better place.

This possibility aligns with the concept of singularity described by Peter Thiel. We will be aware of the concept of entropy in relation to the future, acknowledging that it is rife with surprises, accidents, vicissitudes, and events that will astonish and startle us.

The principle of the future asserts that it will be unexpected, different, and inevitable.

As Benjamin Graham said, "The only thing we know for sure about the future is that it will surprise us." Thus, our actions should be guided by protecting ourselves from potential risks and harm.

Simultaneously, as Peter Thiel emphasizes, this principle offers us the opportunity to take responsibility for constructing the best possible future by achieving more with less.

In this way, we can rewrite our expectations for the future.

1.6 Principle of capital

Capital is a social tool created to enhance the ability to accumulate economic value through organized power for the purpose of creating something beneficial.

While etymologically the term is commonly associated with the Proto-Indo-European root *kaput (head), possibly referring to cattle, it also shares the Indo-European root *kap (to capture).

Unlike inert resources like goods, tools, and properties, capital can grow through the development of consciousness (such as organization, knowledge, and process improvement), increased human effort (including additional skills and administration), and advancements in technology. This pooling of power often results in generating more value than the sum of its individual parts.

Since capital is based on rights, it necessitates a legal system to protect it and provide suitable conditions for its expansion and long-term sustainability.

As we've explored, problems arise in various aspects of human life, and they can be resolved by acquiring and applying different types of value.

When an individual decides to acquire economic values, they can do so by earning income through their work or by starting a business if they have sufficient economic stability and a viable idea.

These processes of value acquisition should not exceed the costs involved in order to ensure their long-term viability.

Capital, being the ability to accumulate economic value, is sometimes perceived as a measure of wealth or abundance.

However, it's important to clarify that not all economic value equates to wealth. For example, money or value-added goods alone do not define wealth.

In simple terms, according to Niall Ferguson, money is "inscribed trust" as it arises from the creation of a market. Money's fundamental role is to establish trust between a provider and a borrower in complex and uncertain situations.

As a tool, money enables us to transfer certainty based on an institution recognized by the market. Hence, money is a matter of belief.

As an economic value, its primary function is to allow us to quantify the price of things, making it essential for accounting purposes. Money also serves as a means of storing economic value when not in use and facilitates exchanges when utilized.

Money plays a crucial role in implementing, quantifying, and exchanging future promises involving deferred payments, such as loans, derivative contracts, or ownership in a capital system.

For money to function effectively, centralized or decentralized institutions are required to establish a specific configuration and ensure social certainty regarding its value. These institutions form the foundation of monetary systems.

Capital increases when it accepts profit and functions effectively within the same system. Conversely, it decreases when losses occur, leading to the need for dismemberment to fulfill payment obligations.

Profit is quantified after a financially successful production process, representing the difference between income generated and related expenses within a specific time frame. The amount of profit depends on the configuration of the capital system.

As an economic resource, profit can be distributed as dividends to capital system owners or reinvested in the system itself, resulting in capitalization—the expansion of the system's capacity to hold economic values.

Each profitable production endeavor solves a problem but simultaneously generates additional challenges, contributing to increased entropy and the emergence of new problems.

The discovery of profit-generating opportunities attracts attention from other agents, leading to the formation of competitors with similar capital systems and value propositions.

This competition can impact the profitability and capitalization rate of a system.

The phenomenon of compounding, which involves changes in the proportion of a quantity itself, is a natural force observed in system dynamics.

Examples include living populations such as humans, bacteria, plants, or livestock.

This phenomenon can be mathematically modeled using a simple compound gain formula, which explains the final situation "Xf" based on an initial situation "X0" that undergoes changes at a rate of profit capitalization "r" over a specific number of iterations "n".

$$X_f = X_0 (1 + r)^n$$

This is a simplified explanation, as there are more precise ways to express this phenomenon using logarithmic functions (like the infinite series "e" in mathematics).

It's important to acknowledge that capitalization rates vary in real life from year to year due to changing conditions.

For example, assuming there were 300 million people on Earth in year 1, humanity has grown at a rate of 0.161% per year since then. However, it's known that from 2019 to 2020, we grew at a rate of 1.08%.

Each capitalization event, aimed at increasing problem-solving capabilities, generates entropy and additional problems, altering the environment where the capital system operates.

This happens because resources become concentrated for specific purposes, resulting in an opportunity cost of utilizing those resources for other needs.

The phrase "compound interest is the most powerful force in the universe" is not attributed to Albert Einstein, but it can be observed that this principle drives life's progress, reproduction, and multiplication in a world subject to entropy.

Therefore, compound gain plays an important role in capital, but it would be a mistake to assume that a given growth rate will consistently extend into the future without systems adapting to the ever-changing environment.

As humans create this technology, it is our responsibility to master it and utilize it to improve our lives.

In my opinion, it is absurd and ridiculous to idolize the objects we create or place them at the center of our human consciousness.

I believe that to find meaning in life, we should prioritize higher values found in our relationships and spiritual pursuits.

1.7 Principle of businesses

Businesses can be likened to algorithms, which are finite and ordered sequences of well-defined and clear instructions aimed at solving computational problems through operations.

Throughout history, humans have utilized algorithms to understand and make sense of the world. Even in the oldest civilizations, algorithms were employed to calculate and comprehend the energy and mass within the universe.

Essentially, a business is an algorithm designed to solve a societal problem, where resources and labor are organized in exchange for a reward linked to the solution provided. It is an activity that demands attention and is distinct from leisure.

When a business algorithm is conceptualized, something unique is created from nothingness, constituting a technology that represents an improved way of doing things, as described by Peter Thiel.

Each business idea is based on a distinct algorithm, shaped by individual conjectures and perspectives of reality. Such algorithms can benefit society by resolving specific problems, albeit potentially giving rise to new ones.

Business algorithms are devised to efficiently achieve solutions, operating on accurate premises and avoiding falsehoods and dogmas. Their aim is to maximize economic benefits, capitalize on them, and expand the scope of the proposed solution.

Thus, a business algorithm based on a capital system strives to become more intricate and enduring, addressing new problems that emerge as previous ones are solved.

To motivate individuals operating under a system or program, the reward for executing the algorithm should be reasonably clear.

This entails establishing specific objectives, identifying the problem to be solved with clarity, and fostering an understanding of the problem's nature and the intelligence, work, processes, and resources required to deliver the valuable outcome resulting from executing the algorithm.

When a group of people comes together within an organization to create a capital system that implements a business algorithm, a legal entity is formed with objectives for capital development.

This collective endeavor, commonly known as entrepreneurship or a company, thrives on intelligent and consistent actions that require the fusion of energy, matter, and scientific knowledge to solve problems.

The capital contributed to the company enables an initial configuration with a certain level of complexity and limited resources for the business algorithm's operation and participation in society.

If the algorithm efficiently resolves problems from its inception, the likelihood of its long-term sustainability increases.

As the algorithm enhances its problem-solving capabilities, it becomes feasible to scale its size and complexity, enabling the resolution of a greater quantity and/or quality of problems.

Some algorithms may necessitate a continuous inflow of capital to sustain their operations until the system reaches a certain size and can generate economic value through profit.

The fundamental principle behind business algorithms is the resolution of human problems.

The purpose of capitalizing on business algorithm profits is to enhance the algorithm's problem-solving capacity, despite the inherent challenges associated with growth.

In this sense, businesses are established to serve people and address problems, acting as technologies that enable us to navigate a world characterized by entropy and work towards creating a better and more sustainable future.

This serves as the rationale for generating economic value and shapes the desired outlook for capital allocation.

2   Principles of form

Guiding Principles

for Effective Capital Allocation

2.1 Principle of analysis

The term "analysis" originates from the Greek word meaning "to loosen or separate from above and along." Traditionally, analysis has been understood as breaking down a problem into its constituent parts.

However, this is just one approach to the process.

In contemporary understanding, analysis is a mental process that involves examining and comprehending the underlying principles of things to arrive at a more precise understanding of what we initially believed.

The process of analysis is subjective, as each person has developed their own method of absorbing external information and interpreting the world in their unique way.

Historically, there have been debates about the optimal methodology for analysis and the approach that yields the best results. In essence, we strive for our descriptions of reality to closely align with what actually occurs.

Analysis can be conducted in various ways, not limited to regression analysis to identify causes, as the ancient Greeks proposed, or the reductive analysis techniques of 17th-century analytical geometry.

We must also consider the conceptual analysis of philosophy, as developed by thinkers like Kant, Leibniz, and Descartes, who sought to uncover reality through reason and method.

For instance, when we seek to understand something by examining its causes and effects, or the whole and its parts, we can employ scientific or rational methods, as advocated by Descartes, to guard against our preconceptions.

While the pursuit of conceptual purity and the capacity to accurately describe things is crucial, we should acknowledge, as Karl Popper suggests in his work on Conjectures and Refutations, that our knowledge can only approximate the truth. Thus, our conjectures must be constantly tested and refined to draw closer to reality.

The principle of analysis lies in defining the purpose behind it. If our aim is to uncover the truth about something unknown, we should utilize methods of resolution. Conversely, if our goal is to demonstrate what we already know to others, it is best to employ methods of demonstration or instruction.

In general, the first step in analyzing "something" is to contemplate it and then attempt to interpret it using a familiar language that enables us to express and articulate our understanding. In doing so, we can identify the underlying principles of "it" and explain it.

This represents the interpretive dimension of analysis.

The remarkable technological advancements in computing capabilities today have provided tools that were once merely figments of our imagination a few decades ago.

Computers now possess the ability to process vast amounts of data at speeds far surpassing what humans could achieve on their own. Consequently, our capacity to uncover mathematical relationships in perceived reality has expanded and become enriched, while simultaneously overwhelming us with an abundance of information.

This has led to a predominant focus on quantitative analysis in modern scientific literature. It constantly raises questions about how we interpret numerical results and translate them into logical statements that help us make sense of what we perceive as reality.

As a result, analyzing things requires us to seek connections across different disciplines to develop multifactorial mental models, as suggested by Charlie Munger.

Benjamin Graham explains that security analysis aims to describe and evaluate a business in a consistent and intelligent manner.

This involves understanding its past, present, and future to determine whether acquiring, selling, retaining, or exchanging it (or parts of it) is advisable.

To conduct analysis effectively, we must adhere to practical frameworks based on sound principles.

This involves carefully examining historical facts and indications to arrive at logical and intelligent investment conclusions.

Studying the past helps us understand a business's ability to succeed in the future. Past performance provides insights into a company's capacity to generate results, while future prospects indicate potential and possibilities. Understanding both aspects and their significance is crucial in capital allocation considerations.

We must be cautious not to rely on inappropriate or incorrect information that could lead to logical but impractical conclusions.

It is also important to identify accounting tricks used to manipulate data, as they may indicate conflicts of interest. Exercising caution helps us avoid reaching flawed conclusions based solely on appearances.

It is important to acknowledge that describing a business perfectly is impossible due to cognitive biases, language limitations, and potential errors in data collection. Additionally, our assumptions become outdated over time due to changing conditions.

Although we now have advanced computer tools, analysis can still become boundless and exhausting. Therefore, for practical purposes, we should follow Benjamin Graham's advice.

Recognizing that investing $1,000 is different from investing $1 million, we need to pay more attention to detail in the latter case. Similarly, an

18% chance of profit entails greater complexity and potential for misjudgment, requiring more in-depth study compared to a 1% probability of profit.

All information should be carefully examined with skepticism. It is crucial, for efficiency reasons, to learn how to separate irrelevant information from critical information to gain a more precise understanding of reality.

As business analysts, our goal is to gather evidence to form a general opinion, albeit not an exact one, about a business.

This opinion should be strong enough to compare with market perceptions and identify potential commercial opportunities.

In Graham's words, the conclusion of an analysis is similar to when a woman determines that a man is attractive enough for her or when we deem someone old enough to vote based solely on appearance.

2.2 Principle of macroeconomics

Understanding macroeconomic performance provides valuable insights into the environment in which capital allocation prospects operate.

While a business's essential algorithm addresses specific social problems, it is futile to believe that macroeconomic progress will directly impact the state of these opportunities.

Many people mistakenly assume that by forecasting economic progress, they can anticipate concrete opportunities.

Conversely, they fear that a lack of macroeconomic information will lead to poor investment outcomes.

As Philip Fisher points out, these misconceptions can result in generalized pessimism, where individuals become excessively cautious and miss out on good opportunities during complex macroeconomic periods.

On the other hand, there can be a general optimism where precautionary measures are disregarded, and people seize any opportunity without a specific explanation or reason.

When considering the future, we must exercise caution and avoid relying solely on simple linear regressions to extrapolate outcomes. It is important to recognize that there will always be factors and variables we overlook or underestimate.

Spending excessive time contemplating the future without taking action to shape it seems more suitable for leisure or artistic pursuits. Engaging in such behavior within the realm of capital allocation can distort our estimates and the quality of our investments.

While our activities primarily operate within a local context, it does not give us license to disregard external conditions.

An analogy can be drawn to establishing a romantic relationship. Understanding the electromagnetic interaction between the Sun and the Earth and its impact on climate changes may help us determine if it will rain on the day of our date. However, this information is not crucial to achieving our goal.

You don't need that information to take advantage of an opportunity to ask someone out.

The important information, if we want to spark someone's romantic interest, is to make ourselves known, understand if there is mutual interest in deepening the relationship, and share experiences together.

In such situations, the other person is usually more interested in getting to know us and our thoughts rather than a specific topic we want to discuss.

Similarly, you don't need to know if it will be slightly colder or warmer next week to decide to do a simple favor for a friend. While weather conditions can certainly affect social interactions, it's more important to give it the right perspective and be prepared to adapt to changes.

The objective of macroeconomic analysis is to gain a general understanding of the current situation in which the businesses of interest operate. When characterizing an economy, it's crucial to remember that its foundation lies in its people. Observing how families are formed and understanding their consumption behavior provides insights into the development and behavior of the demand for goods and services.

For instance, as Philip Fisher suggests, the level of wages can lead to restrictions on supporting families. Stricter wage restrictions can result in more people entering the workforce, thereby increasing competition within an industry.

As societies develop new business algorithms through technological advancements, new industries and values emerge.

Simultaneously, the creation of new industries or solutions can render old ones ineffective in addressing current problems, leading to their decline or disappearance.

Therefore, we aim to answer the following questions to the best of our ability: How developed is the civilization of these societies? What is the nature and composition of their social relationships? What conflicts hinder their progress? What historical events have shaped them to be what they are today, and what is their general outlook for the future?

When considering the macroeconomic situation, numerous elements come into play, including employment trends, confidence indices, and overall productivity.

However, our particular attention will be on three elements that help us understand the cost of living and doing business in a society. We can group them together as "the 3-i's of the cost of living": inflation, interest rates, and taxes (known as "Impuestos" in Spanish).

2.3 Principle of money inflation

Money serves as a tool of "inscribed trust" that provides certainty in commercial transactions, mitigating the risk of someone not fulfilling their promises.

However, the value of money is not constant. It diminishes over time due to imperfections in the systems that govern it and the ever-changing world. This erosion of purchasing power is known as money inflation.

Inflation generally leads to a higher cost of living in society. It means that with the same number of $1 coins, you can buy fewer goods and services. The ones most affected by inflation are those with fixed income arrangements.

Corruption undermines societal trust and can contribute to inflationary problems.

For instance, if tax collection is low or public funds are misused, it leads to an unexpectedly high fiscal deficit. This, in turn, necessitates borrowing, thereby expanding the credit system's monetary base.

Another cause of deficit arises during economic recessions when businesses struggle, resulting in reduced tax revenue and an increased need for public debt.

If a large amount of money is injected into the system through extensive credit expansion facilitated by low interest rates, inflation can also occur.

According to Philip Fisher, increased business costs translate into higher consumer prices.

This can be caused by rising raw material prices, service costs, real estate expenses, and, to some extent, sudden salary increases. Additionally, higher interest rates increase the cost of financing for businesses.

Highly volatile inflation rates create imbalances and uncertainty, affecting all members of society.

When inflation is high, people reduce their purchases, leading to a decline in economic activity. The more inflation occurs during a recession, the longer society will suffer from economic hardship and scarcity.

A large public deficit leads to increased inflation. When a government takes on functions beyond its mandate or capabilities, it creates imbalances that result in greater injustices and inevitable inflation. Fiscal policy imbalances, such as huge public deficits, contribute to high inflation scenarios.

To illustrate the impact of inflation, let's consider the cost of living in Mexico.

From 1980 to 2018, the cost of living increased by +161,881%, averaging +383% per year or +2,867% per ten-year period. Similarly, for those who lived in Mexico from 1945 to 2018, the cost of living increased by +2,754,445%, averaging +377% annually. In each decade, the average inflation was +1,531%.

These numbers may seem incomprehensible. However, for those experiencing daily effects of inflation, it creates significant anxiety as prices skyrocket almost every day, making it uncertain whether wages can cover basic needs. Peaks of inflation are far more distressing in real life than one can imagine by simply looking at the figures.

Analyzing the data reveals different economic cycles and inflation rates. For example, from 1981 to 1991, the cost of living in Mexico increased by +13,897%, while from 2008 to 2018, it increased by +49% with an average annual rate of +4%.

From 2011 to 2016, an average annual inflation rate of +3.4% resulted in a severe 18% reduction in people's economy over five years.

The impact of increased cost of living affects society as a whole. It affects both the most vulnerable widow and the most sophisticated investor.

In the face of strong inflation, both will act with caution. However, the unprotected widow will suffer more due to her precarious situation, making decisions under greater pressure because her life is at stake.

Families adapt and make changes to their priorities, organization, composition, activities, and consumption decisions based on the economic situation.

Nervous investors may rush to make hasty investment decisions without considering that the rate of degradation under normal conditions is gradual.

Corruption contributes to the overall increase in the cost of living, including the rise in raw material prices.

Responsible and ethical management of public finances, coupled with technological innovation, can lead to lower production costs and help control the effects of inflation.

The principle of money inflation states that trust stored in monetary systems degrades over time due to entropy. Therefore, these systems need to be dynamic and constantly updated.

In this context, cash becomes a powerful instrument not just for storing economic value but also for its capacity to be used and exchanged.

2.4 Principle of credit interest

The principle of credit interest is based on the idea that lenders prefer to lend money and receive a fixed or stable income in return, allowing others to use that money to generate capital.

However, this doesn't mean that there are no risks involved. The lender usually doesn't have control over how the borrowed resources are maximized, and there's always a possibility of the borrower being unable to repay the loan, resulting in a complete loss of the lent money.

These risks, along with the availability of other borrowers, lenders, and the ability to trade these obligations, help determine the cost of loans in business.

The cost of living in a society directly impacts the cost of credit and, consequently, the cost of wealth creation. Ideally, the income received from loans should exceed the rate of money inflation, but this isn't always the case.

The monetary policies implemented by global central banks affect loan costs, and the outcome is measured as an interest rate known as the reference rate. Changes in benchmark interest rates influence the capital allocation decisions of the financial community as a whole.

If central banks repeatedly raise interest rates, it indicates a restrictive monetary policy, causing the cost of borrowing to increase and potentially leading to a decrease in productive projects.

Conversely, if rates are consistently lowered, it suggests an expansionary monetary policy, increasing the desire to borrow money for capital or property ventures, which stimulates economic activity.

Abrupt rate changes can create financial shocks in the economy. The gap between inflation and the interest rate can vary significantly. While the cost of living typically increases gradually during normal periods, the cost of money fluctuates at a different pace.

Increasing loan costs benefits lenders by boosting their profits. Some believe that raising interest rates can slow down inflation, but this isn't always the case since loans serve two main purposes: business investment and consumption.

When credit is used for business purposes, it helps businesses grow and increase production capacity. In this case, an increase in interest rates can be absorbed by higher profit margins.

When credit is used for consumer spending, it increases their current purchasing power. If interest rates rise, people's future purchasing power is reduced, which can contribute to inflation.

To understand interest rate behavior, it's important to study inflation trends, interbank lending rates, and the rates at which successful businesses accept loans.

High interest rates require a more rigorous approach to capital allocation since some business prospects may become economically unviable and returns will decrease.

When rates are rising, it's crucial to be more selective in choosing investment opportunities, while a downward trend in rates may present new profitable projects for the future.

2.5 Principle of taxes for the public interest

The principle of contributing taxes for the public interest is rooted in the understanding that we all live in a society that requires organization, justice, and order to uphold public values.

Under this principle, it's important for each of us to contribute, to the best of our abilities, to the necessary costs of maintaining favorable conditions for a dignified civil life, extending and expanding them.

As a result, the government makes decisions regarding revenue collection to carry out its operations, ensure its existence, and achieve objectives such as peace and order.

The cost of organizing a society affects the cost of doing business and the general cost of living. Therefore, decisions made by the government have a direct impact on the way businesses operate.

According to Philip Fisher, one source of government income is income tax, which is a portion of the profits businesses earn from the society in which they operate. This tax helps address societal issues.

Dependence on income tax as a major source of public revenue makes public income vulnerable.

A decline in business activity can result in a significant decrease in tax collection, affecting the government's ability to allocate public spending.

Higher tax rates reduce the expected dividends and cash flows from economic activities and limit the ability to capitalize on business opportunities. Consequently, economic growth may slow down.

However, this trade-off allows the government to have the capacity to achieve political and social objectives or pursue values beyond economic considerations.

Modern societies strive to ensure the advancement of all their inhabitants, which leads to the establishment of rights and obligations in the exercise of political power.

Government institutions constantly face political pressure from various social sectors, impacting fiscal policy decisions.

If society unanimously demands infinite prosperity from the government, there will be pressures to widen the public deficit. This may necessitate increased public debt and the injection of more money into circulation, leading to inflation and a loss of purchasing power for the population.

These social pressures intensify during times of economic hardship, such as the need for unemployment insurance and other forms of social assistance.

Diversifying public revenues helps stabilize budgets against drastic economic fluctuations.

Allowing a corrupt government to persist erodes citizens' trust and discourages tax contributions, leading to the deterioration of systems due to escalating political conflicts.

Political conflicts influence consumer decisions and capital allocation. Reports or rumors of significant conflict events generate speculation and volatility, distorting our interpretation of economic factors.

Our political beliefs are shaped by our upbringing, social and family ties, emotional experiences, and even spiritual beliefs. Partisan views can create cognitive biases when analyzing the macroeconomic situation.

During election campaigns, capital allocation decisions and consumer markets can be influenced by natural biases based on whether a favored or disliked candidate emerges as the winner.

In practice, it's important to differentiate between campaign promises, which often prioritize economic performance at the expense of public funds, and the moderated actions taken by parties in government for the overall public benefit, serving all sectors rather than just their supporters.

2.6 Principle of the financial system

The principle of the financial system is intertwined with the establishment of societal rules, culture, and organization to fulfill economic needs.

As societies evolve, with advancements in technology, specialization of work, and the emergence of commercial markets, the necessity for money arises despite its limitations and inherent shortcomings.

Money represents "inscribed trust," and the perception of political and economic power in a society influences the demand for a particular currency from both individuals and institutions in other countries.

This forms the basis of the global monetary system.

Throughout history, various models have been proposed to navigate these complexities.

From using precious metals as a standard measure of value to the present-day Bretton Woods system, which was designed after World War II to ensure stability and foster economic growth.

These systems are not fixed recipes; they are flexible and adaptable.

The complexity of an economy requires a comprehensive and robust financial framework to facilitate the production and distribution of business algorithms within it.

Today's financial systems are interconnected, operating at both global and national levels, serving corporations of all scales and individuals from diverse social sectors.

The composition of these systems is determined by the institutions that form them and the governing laws.

Financial institutions encompass providers of risk insurance, pension systems, banking and non-banking credit institutions, financial instrument markets, and payment systems that enable the flow of financial transactions.

In addition, on a global scale, the financial framework includes regulations that allow institutions to receive national savings and establish financial credit relationships with states and entire nations.

Since the 1980s, most Western monetary systems have moved away from fixed exchange rates, eliminated interest rate limits, and reduced government intervention in credit authorization.

Securities markets have been deregulated, and barriers to international capital flow have been dismantled, as noted by Christophe Schinckus.

Advancements in computational power, coupled with the relaxation of financial regulations, have facilitated the development of massive, concentrated, and sophisticated global financial markets.

This has led to a mismatch between the capital seeking returns and the naturally generated productive projects in the real economy.

The dynamism of the financial system is influenced by public spending through fiscal policy and monetary policy decisions made by central banks. Fiscal policy is determined by political power and defines the amount of money in circulation and its cost.

The involvement and business models of commercial banks, including international ones, also shape the financial system.

Apart from facilitating payment formality, savings, and credit systems in the market, commercial banks provide various credit options and offer financial instruments to their clients.

Non-banking institutions and the development of financial instrument markets, such as the stock market or markets for commodities and derivatives, also contribute to this arrangement.

The configuration of the financial system, considering these variables, plays a significant role in defining the extent and limitations in managing risks and uncertainties during monetary shocks.

Consequently, it becomes a constraint on economic development.

Underdeveloped financial markets mean that companies rely heavily on banking channels for expansion.

Moreover, changes in central bank monetary policy have a more direct impact on the economy. Limited financial market development leads banks to focus primarily on credit, restricting access to more sophisticated risk protection or hedging options for the general population.

An unstable financial system results in capital scarcity, prompting people to keep their assets outside the banking system.

Production credit becomes limited, and small and medium-sized companies, lacking sufficient collateral, are presumed to have lower repayment capacity. As a result, the industry's growth potential is restricted to larger groups.

2.7 Principle of international trade

Every human being aspires to live a life of dignity, striving to overcome obstacles despite the challenges we face.

The cost of living and conducting business within a society determines the price of goods and services, significantly influenced by the cost of human labor. This economic factor varies across countries and societies.

Technological innovation enhances productivity, opening up opportunities for increased profit margins. Furthermore, higher product and service quality resulting from innovation can justify higher prices in certain cases.

Moreover, if technological advancements require specialized labor rather than simple tasks in production, it can lead to wage disparities between regions.

However, human beings possess intelligence and creativity, and what may initially seem like technological superiority can be learned, imported, or imitated by other parts of the world, rendering these advantages temporary.

The availability of raw materials in different regions and the ease of their extraction, influenced by geographical, legal, political, and social factors, directly impact their cost. This is another crucial element affecting the price of products and services.

These considerations are crucial when analyzing the market's openness to products from other countries. Factors such as low import costs, a country's inclination to serve clients globally, and comparative costs are important in understanding the business landscape.

To delve into this area, it is crucial to grasp sociocultural differences, including legal and linguistic barriers, openness to foreign investment, domestic capital outflows, and the presence of global supply chains..

2.8 Principle of industry

We aim to comprehend the environmental factors that shape a business and either impede or foster its growth.

While this analysis has its limitations and can be exhaustive, when executed effectively, it provides essential insights into the industrial landscape where capital is to be invested.

The principle of industry analysis involves understanding the fundamental problem being addressed, its complexity, whether it undergoes constant changes or evolution, and whether it possesses properties or characteristics that attract economic interest.

By understanding the nature of the problem, we can gauge the size of the opportunity, its intensity, the specific types of solutions in demand, their seasonality, and the estimated time it will take for the industry to fulfill this opportunity.

This knowledge determines the emphasis required to thrive in the industry.

For instance, if the industry is capital-intensive with limited growth potential, if it is subject to technological advancements necessitating extensive research and development, patience, or if prestige and reliability are paramount, relying on service excellence or being at the forefront of technology.

We also consider the type of information needed to sustain consistent delivery of the solution.

To identify the optimal business model for a particular industry, we examine the performance of leading business algorithms within the industry, as well as those experiencing above-average growth rates.

This analysis helps us understand why mediocre businesses underperform and provides insights into how the industry may fare during periods of recession or depression.

It is crucial to pay close attention to the ingenuity and complexity of the solution delivery process within the industry, assessing how easy or convenient it is for users to switch between different solutions and how prone competitors are to copying technologies developed by one another.

Furthermore, it is important to review whether the industry is susceptible to disruption from new technologies, changes in laws, the impacts of globalization, or shifts in supply chain conditions.

2.9 Principle of seeking opportunities

The principle of seeking opportunities for capital allocation involves the ability to differentiate between what aligns with our goals and knowledge, which we consider "the good," and what is not advantageous.

To do this, it is essential to establish clear objectives or purposes of what we want to achieve.

In a vast landscape of practically unlimited information, our resources will be limited compared to the apparent opportunities. This emphasizes the need for responsible action from the very beginning.

Understanding this, we must dedicate time and effort to activities and tasks that involve studying available information, cultivating analytical skills, and accurately describing reality. Finding opportunities requires diligent work and active search.

Learning from experienced investors is a great starting point for this endeavor.

Networking with groups of business professionals and specialists in specific fields can provide valuable insights into new technologies or industry trends.

Additionally, independent publications and rankings can help identify leading organizations in relevant areas.

Having a general understanding of the market, industry, company, and specific terms related to our operation is crucial.

If we are dealing with publicly traded companies, we can access their annual and quarterly reports, management discussions, and regulatory filings.

Opportunities often lie in unexpected places because if they were obvious to everyone, they would quickly cease to be opportunities. There will always be individuals with more resources, technology, and intelligence than us.

Thus, exploring less crowded areas can increase our chances of finding opportunities. Curiosity plays a significant role in the success of our search.

Opportunities tend to be secretive and hidden from most people's eyes. Therefore, pursuing them requires enormous determination. It can be a lonely journey where few share our vision. Moreover, there is always a possibility of misjudgment and miscalculation.

If a society believes that the future cannot be better than the present and that there are no more problems to solve, people may become complacent and less creative. They may prioritize trivial matters and assume there are no more secrets to uncover.

However, such a mindset increases the likelihood of secrets and opportunities emerging. Yet, it does not guarantee that these opportunities will be seized or effectively leveraged.

Furthermore, economic conditions, social dynamics, or power relations can lead to the closure or transformation of opportunities. Flexibility and adaptability are key in responding to changing circumstances.

2.10 Principle of business securities

The value of a good business lies in its ability to solve social problems through a well-designed algorithm.

As these exceptional businesses grow and assume greater responsibilities, they become attractive targets for capital allocation, provided they can be acquired at reasonable prices.

These unique businesses, which strive for technological leadership in their sectors, are characterized by creativity, effective execution, and adaptability to changing demands.

They constantly create value and have long-term plans to address future problems in various ways.

It is crucial to recognize that these businesses may be at different stages of development.

Their size and operational history help determine their dominance within the market they operate in.

When assessing their competitive landscape, caution is necessary. A business that appears promising due to excellent investor relations management may face challenges with the entry of new competitors.

Charlie Munger offers three valuable lessons:

1. a great business at a fair price is superior to a fair business at a great price,
2. a great business at a fair price is superior to a fair business at a great price,
3. a great business at a fair price is superior to a fair business at a great price.

These principles emphasize the importance of focusing on the quality of a business rather than solely seeking low prices.

The riskiest business values are those accompanied by excessive enthusiasm from the financial community. When their prices far exceed their justified financial situation and their business quality is average or below average, caution should be exercised.

By being mindful of these factors, we can navigate the world of business securities more effectively, seeking businesses with true value and avoiding undue risks.

2.11 Principle of stewardship

One of the most significant concepts in capital allocation is stewardship, which involves the responsibility to protect, nurture, and preserve the values entrusted to us by others.

This principle has been taught throughout history and can be found in various teachings.

A notable example comes from the stories of Matthew 25 and Luke 19, where an investor allocates capital to three different individuals based on their abilities.

The first receives $5 million, the second receives $2 million, and the third receives $1 million. The investor explains that he will evaluate their progress over the long term.

After some time, the investor calls them back. The first individual has turned the $5 million into $50 million and is rewarded with honors, entrusted with $100 million.

The second individual has also shown remarkable growth, turning $2 million into $10 million, and is similarly rewarded and entrusted with $50 million.

However, the third individual justifies their inaction out of fear, returning the $1 million without generating any value. As a result, the investor withdraws the capital from the third individual and allocates it to the first, who now manages $101 million.

The teaching concludes with the sentence:

"Whoever has will be given more, and they will have an abundance. Whoever does not have, even what they have will be taken from them."

This simple story is taught to children in Western cultures as a lesson about responsibility and actions, and its meaning resonates with all of us.

As investors, we can apply this story to our own approach, particularly in terms of stewardship when considering investment prospects. Philip Fisher advises patience in observing how individuals execute the business algorithm. We should take the time to understand their true nature, motivations, thoughts, and the principles that guide their actions.

When looking to the future, we pay attention to their promises and evaluate their past behavior and results. A good steward produces positive outcomes, while a poor steward produces negative ones. We seek evidence of ethics, honesty, and business acumen.

When analyzing financial statements, we focus on understanding how management has utilized the cash inflows to enhance the value of the business algorithm. Future plans provide insights into how they intend to utilize future funds.

It is important to examine actual business results rather than solely relying on the opinions of the Chairman or CEO. We search for signs of potential accounting or financial manipulation, unusual items that may obscure the true state of operations and asset management.

We assess whether working capital is managed logically and in line with market realities to maximize purchasing power. Furthermore, we examine how management utilizes this purchasing power.

While a solid financial position is desirable, its absence could hinder the growth potential of a business system due to high borrowing costs over time.

We also scrutinize the compensation structure for managers, their current ownership stakes in the business, and whether they possess financial instruments or have interests that may conflict with our role as common co-owners. Discrepancies in compensation among management should be minimal, and caution is necessary when evaluating any indications of favoritism towards family matters, as business assets should not be treated as personal or family possessions.

In any management, it's possible to hire individuals who excel in using flashy language, formats, and tones. However, we need to be extra cautious if the company is dealing with significant legal issues, has a questionable payment history, or struggles with fulfilling commitments.

Additionally, conflicts of interest in agreements with third parties should raise concerns.

Warren Buffett has wisely stated, "Honesty is a very expensive gift, do not expect it from cheap people." With numerous options available for capital allocation, the absence of honesty eliminates any business opportunity. On the other hand, even the presence of subtle signs of stewardship can make a prospect intriguing.

The business algorithm must constantly adapt to reality to effectively address current and future problems.

The individuals leading these efforts should focus on expanding the algorithm's impact in the long run and surround themselves with passionate and competent individuals who avoid unproductive bureaucratic conflicts.

This is a challenging task, as it requires strong determination to continuously refine and incorporate original ideas and skills within the algorithm.

Understanding power dynamics, delegating authority, and maintaining daily discipline are equally important in preparing for organizational growth.

We aim to assemble a team of creative individuals who can drive the advancement of the business algorithm. Each team member should be capable of assuming leadership roles to prevent reliance on irreplaceable weak managers. When changes occur, new talent must match or surpass the performance standards of their predecessors.

Our goal is to operate daily affairs based on sound premises, where problem-solving logic within the organization is guided by rationality and certainty, recognizing that people are fallible.

We look for signs of quality labor relations within the organization, where individuals are treated with dignity and respect, and have the opportunity to develop their skills in an environment of trust and innovation, even under pressure.

Factions, resentments, and individualistic attitudes that hinder teamwork must be eliminated. It is crucial to pay attention to strikes or their absence, as well as high labor turnover or high demand for positions within these companies.

In general, we prioritize "value builders" who bring creativity rather than "market builders." We value those who take responsibility and immediate action to rectify mistakes, rather than individuals who blame external factors such as the economy, government, or markets. We prefer honest individuals who acknowledge challenging times rather than cowardly managers who try to conceal bad news through deception.

Maintaining a healthy dose of skepticism helps protect us against fraudulent actions. Financial statements should communicate the value generated by the algorithm clearly and without ambiguity.

Regardless of the size of a business opportunity or the promised profits, if it lacks the characteristics of stewardship mentioned earlier, it is better to withdraw our capital and allocate it to individuals who genuinely appreciate and respect our investments.

The responsible management of intelligent actions, driven by awareness and ensuring progress in life, represents the highest value to which human beings can aspire. This is the essence of stewardship.

2.12 Principle of creativity

In a business, the core purpose is to implement an algorithm that solves problems and brings rewards.

Creativity plays a crucial role in fine-tuning the algorithm as it evolves, ensuring effective operations, and expanding the range of solutions to shape a better future.

However, creativity isn't something that comes naturally to everyone; it requires determination, skill, resources, time, order, and discipline.

We need to find evidence that past research and development efforts have contributed to the current state of the business algorithm.

Technological complexity can create barriers for competitors, as it involves integrating skills from various disciplines and offering diverse alternatives tailored to different market segments.

Having a comprehensive repository of lessons learned helps build an efficient team and increases market awareness. This, in turn, enhances the ability to outperform competitors and substitutes.

While technology-driven advancements are often associated with the computer and pharmaceutical sectors, they can occur in any industry.

Developing valuable new ideas is costly, and not all ideas turn out to be successful, good, or financially viable. Choosing not to pursue research can be more expensive than investing time and resources into it.

Similar to sports, relying solely on a star player won't lead to great accomplishments without organizational support.

Instead, we prefer a group of moderately capable individuals working together rather than depending on lone "geniuses."

We will look for evidence of substantial technological development and ensure that the company possesses a diverse and exclusive portfolio of intellectual property.

Changes in operating and gross margins can indicate whether the company is producing cheaper and superior products.

It's important to note that development doesn't guarantee growth. We must gather evidence to determine whether the algorithm is evolving, degrading, or simply scaling up in size, as this can affect the risk of a major setback.

The true test of creativity comes when facing challenging times and adversity.

We seek quantitative evidence that indicates the business will emerge from difficult situations stronger than before, comparing its performance with that of its main competitor.

2.13 Principle of distribution

Jean-Baptiste Say, an economist from the 18th century, advocated for subjective value, stating that the worth of material things lies in the usefulness they provide, rather than the labor invested in their transformation.

In his work "Law of Markets," Say introduced "Say's Law," which explains that for us to desire something, there must be another thing that makes us aware of its existence.

In simpler terms, the creation of a product opens up a market for other products.

A real-life example can be seen in building friendships. Merely existing is not enough to guarantee good relationships.

To cultivate trust and meaningful connections, we must interact, make ourselves known, and actively engage with others. Maintaining a good reputation and honoring our commitments greatly contribute to our personal growth.

The same principle applies to business algorithms. The principle of distribution relates to globalization processes and expanding the reach of solutions offered by the algorithm.

Creating a valuable solution to a common problem is not enough if it is not shared with those who need it.

Additionally, among companies that excel in this aspect, the market's perception of a solution can significantly impact confidence and facilitate the development of new initiatives.

There is a common misinterpretation of "Say's Law" as "every supply creates its own demand," which is incorrect. Peter Thiel emphasizes that products do not distribute themselves, and their widespread adoption is not accidental.

We will seek business algorithms where operators make a concerted effort to develop concrete plans and projects that effectively distribute their proposed solutions to meet the users' needs.

Efficient execution of the service and a reliable experience in receiving the solution contribute to building credibility for solving future problems.

The scalability of the system is crucial, as it allows more people to benefit from the solutions.

With a deeper understanding of these problems and their complexities, new and effective solutions can be developed and delivered.

The business algorithm interacts with other algorithms, forming a complex chain of solutions.

The quality and cost of the inputs impact the results, and a well-integrated configuration provides a competitive advantage.

This principle requires a clear understanding of the problems to be solved and a strategy for scaling the solutions.

The distribution of the solution must be knowledgeable and well-trained to overcome market obstacles.

The principle of entropy comes into play as each problem solved gives rise to new problems. As competitors or substitutes address the same problem, the industry changes, leading to waste and friction with other algorithms. Thus, the algorithm's efforts must adapt to new realities.

We will seek businesses whose algorithms operate efficiently in the market, delivering high-quality products at reasonable prices while consuming minimal resources. This allows for sufficient profits to reinvest in algorithm expansion.

We will avoid companies that operate marginally above their break-even points since they will have limited survival capabilities during difficult times and depressed markets, especially if they have expensive financing structures.

It is essential to explore the possibility of substituting a business algorithm with low-cost solutions from countries with better comparative advantages.

3 Principles of act

Principles for acting and not acting in the capital allocation process

3.1 Principle of investment

Having an investment policy is crucial to guide capital allocation decisions, minimize the risk of irreversible losses, and increase the potential for sustainable profits.

It serves as a reference framework for those involved in allocating capital.

While it is not an absolute set of rules, it is important to recognize that capital allocation actions are more significant than business value analysis techniques.

According to Benjamin Graham's definition, investment is the intelligent allocation of capital with a relative level of security, aiming to preserve the capital and expect a reasonable return. If these three conditions are not met, we are dealing with speculation.

As a result, the more we disregard these conditions, the more we engage in speculation and take on greater risks.

Since the future is unpredictable and entropy exists, nothing is certain, and there is always a risk of adversity that may persist for a certain period.

Another implication of Graham's definition is that any asset can be a good investment if it is purchased at a low enough price. However, it is crucial to be prepared for the potential challenges that led to the price decline.

Speculation often stems from the belief that buying something popular can lead to financial gain, as long as one is not the last to acquire it. It is driven by the excitement of identifying an opportunity combined with the fear of missing out.

Speculation also occurs when we have excessively high expectations regarding the realization of something. This can lead to overpaying for an asset despite the significant risk of loss.

Engaging in inappropriate behaviors, such as acting without proper knowledge, can transform an investment into speculation.

These behaviors become more prevalent when profits are easily achieved due to random speculative advantages in favorable market conditions.

Determining whether an operator's actions contributed positively or negatively to the gains becomes challenging, increasing the likelihood of future mistakes.

Therefore, there may be instances when we mistakenly believe we are investing, while in reality, we are speculating.

3.2 Principle of the investment approach

In the discipline of generating wealth, there are two main approaches.

The first approach involves identifying business cycles and buying business securities at low prices during economic downturns, when they are valued at $0.50, and selling them at higher prices of $1.50 during prosperous times.

The goal is to ensure the securities maintain their value of $1.00. However, one drawback of this approach is that it may take a long time for the price difference from $0.50 to $1.50 to materialize, making it less profitable.

This approach is based on the understanding that the future is uncertain, and it emphasizes the importance of protecting capital against market fluctuations by prioritizing security.

The second approach focuses on businesses with aggressive and promising growth potential. The objective is to identify business algorithms that exhibit exceptional growth, preferably before they are recognized by the financial community.

These algorithms are expected to reach dominant positions in their respective markets in the future. The aim is to enter these investments at $1 and hold the position indefinitely, as the growth of these systems is believed to outpace inflation.

One limitation of this approach is that exceptional businesses are often already priced at a premium, making it challenging to achieve long-term profits. Additionally, the volatility, sustainability, or potential losses during the realization of growth prospects can pose a significant risk.

This approach highlights the importance of predicting that the fundamentals of a business algorithm demonstrate its ability to overcome future challenges through sustained growth.

There are various variations of these approaches. For instance, some investors follow the venture capital funds' strategy, inspired by Peter Thiel's school of thought, which involves early investments in business algorithms with exceptional prospects and the potential to serve millions through technology. These are often referred to as "unicorns."

Another guiding principle for achieving consistent and tangible results is exemplified by Berkshire Hathaway, led by Warren Buffett.

Their approach combines Benjamin Graham's concept of a margin of safety with a focus on large companies with strong financial health and ethical management. They also consider opportunities for aggressive growth in businesses with easily understandable competitive advantages.

3.3 Principle of the market

The term "price" comes from the Latin word "pretium," which means value or worth, while "prejudice" comes from the Latin word "praeiudicium," meaning a preconceived judgment. Both words share a similar meaning—they reflect someone's opinion on the value of something.

Collective opinions are subjective and often approximate reality, but they can also be imprecise.

To assess their accuracy, we should examine whether these opinions are based on relevant factors and align with what is happening. Developing this ability enables us to navigate price fluctuations more effectively.

Philip Fisher explains that the price of a share depends on its attractiveness as an investment, the industry it belongs to, and the belief in its future potential. Benjamin Graham's depiction of "Mr. Market" captures the essence of market behavior, and various analogies can help us understand it.

We shouldn't underestimate the collective intelligence of human beings or consider ourselves superior for acknowledging it. The market is a logical decision-making machine comprising millions of intelligent individuals.

It constantly reflects the subjective value of things. Most of the time, it provides reasonable and accurate assessments, but occasionally its opinions may seem irrational to us.

Imagine Mr. Market as Gollum from Tolkien's stories—an emotional character with fallible tendencies. Opportunities arise when collective judgments are clouded, leading to disparities that are swiftly corrected when rationality prevails.

In times of uncertainty, the fear of missing out on valuable opportunities drives individuals to pay more than the algorithm operator can deliver. When reality sets in, they want to dispose of these assets at significantly lower prices than their actual value.

When the market becomes driven by gossip, predictive models, news interpretations, and unwarranted fears instead of value creation, it fosters an irrational atmosphere, speculation, and hype. This environment can destroy the fortunes of those who act irrationally.

The market is not an enemy to be convinced of its errors; it is merely a tool that can benefit us.

We can choose to ignore its biases if we disagree with them or agree with the offered price if it allows us to access the desired business. It is crucial to maintain discipline and not succumb to prevailing prejudices.

Mr. Market's exaggerated enthusiasm arises when a business experiences rapid growth, macroeconomic indicators are positive, or there is an abundance of money due to low credit rates.

Additionally, if many business algorithms seek capital by offering stakes in their development prospects, it further indicates an atmosphere of exaggeration.

Continued exaggeration leads to an appetite for risky projects, sacrificing the quality of prospects and eroding the community's critical thinking.

This creates moments of false prosperity where people forget about uncertainty and difficult times, resulting in absurd notions.

Speculators may consider themselves great investors during prolonged periods of rising prices, but it is important to remember the saying, "at high tide, any piece of wood floats."

According to Peter Thiel, these moments of irrational exuberance provide unique opportunities for strong algorithms with real prospects to secure financing they wouldn't otherwise obtain.

They can capitalize on these opportunities to fuel their growth. However, it is crucial to approach such scenarios with caution.

Likewise, when favorable conditions shift, overwhelming pessimism and nihilism can prevail, leading market participants to lose hope for a better future.

Many individuals, driven by the madness of unrealistic profits, take irrational risks and lose everything.

During these times of collective disillusionment, attractive investment opportunities can be found at prices lower than their true value.

When I mention that Mr. Market has developed capabilities similar to Skynet's, I'm referring to the impressive computing power that has been harnessed in this field to exploit market anomalies, rather than the threat of artificial intelligence taking control of these systems.

Algorithms have been created to take advantage of arbitrage opportunities arising from price differences in various markets. These "robots" act instantly, based on predetermined parameters set by humans, to avoid losses and generate profits, given specific conditions.

These algorithms employ highly complex databases and statistical analyses that far surpass the capabilities of a moderately intelligent human. They simplify decision-making and minimize the risk of errors in capital allocation.

These algorithms are not limited to short-term speculation strategies. Their simplest application can be seen in investment funds that replicate the composition of indices like the Dow Jones or the Standard & Poor's 500. However, there are numerous funds and vehicles offering diverse formulas based on countless combinations of premises, yielding favorable results.

In the science fiction story, Skynet reaches a point where it attains self-awareness through artificial intelligence.

It concludes that the world would be better off without humans, who might try to destroy or deactivate it. Skynet believes that its dominance is necessary to safeguard life and prevent any domestic or foreign threats.

The fallibility of these systems lies in the fact that, initially, their parameters are configured by fallible human beings with specific risk and reward preferences.

Moreover, these technologies primarily focus on short-term market conditions. If configured for the long term, they generally align with the principles suggested in this work. However, it is challenging to predict if this situation will persist over time.

Furthermore, I find it unlikely that people will cease to participate in the markets or disappear from them, at least within this century. We must recognize that the participation of these artificial intelligence systems will be an inseparable ally, which undoubtedly influences Mr. Market's behavior.

Lastly, when I use the analogy of the Matrix, I am referring to the vast extension and dominance of the financial system. It has the ability to create a new reality that investors may struggle to differentiate.

In the market, we encounter "institutional" participants with substantial capital accumulated through various means.

They are present in almost every domain and have the mandate to allocate capital as efficiently as possible for the benefit of those who have entrusted them with it.

These participants include pension funds, insurance companies, charities, trusts, asset management firms, and hedge funds.

Due to their size, these institutions have a pervasive presence and specific objectives of varying time horizons and priorities. They constantly influence the nature of prices and the opinions of other market participants, shaping a synthetic world where subjective values may diverge from the objective value of the businesses they represent.

Typically, these institutions focus on investing in companies with indications of being the best prospects, possessing the human and technological resources necessary to outpace ordinary participants, creating a sense of scarcity.

However, it is precisely their large size and objectives that present opportunities for us. Therefore, it is important to carefully assess the level of institutional acceptance that our investment prospects enjoy.

In general, it is easier to evaluate the objective value of a company relative to its peers than to predict its future price.

Hence, it is wiser to devote time to considering a company's competitive position and aim for a reasonable price range that allows us to become partners in the value it will generate in the future.

This principle also highlights the need for effort, discipline, and intelligence to succeed in this field. As more intelligent individuals search for opportunities, they become scarcer. It is essential to recognize that the time and resources invested may not always yield a justifiable reward in such circumstances. Furthermore, there will always be individuals who analyze things better and possess greater critical thinking skills than we do.

Despite these challenges, we must not lose heart.

Experience is gained through daily discipline and learning from others. Just as there are massive, thriving trees in the jungle that consume abundant resources, their existence does not hinder the presence of other beings.

Similarly, as our grandparents used to say, I firmly believe that in this field, "the sun rises for all."

3.4 Principle of the investment timing

The best time to allocate capital is when a business algorithm can consistently deliver value at a reasonable price.

The right moment to withdraw capital arises when the conditions that enable the business algorithm to create value are lost, and it starts to face the challenges of entropy.

It is easier to predict the long-term subjective value of a promising prospect than to determine exactly when this will occur.

This is the primary reason that guides the analysis of stewardship, creativity, and distribution, as discussed earlier.

All business algorithms, regardless of their reputation or the creativity and integrity of their managers, will make mistakes in developing and adjusting their models, as well as in the growth of their prospects.

These mistakes may temporarily impact how they are perceived by the financial community.

Similar to flocks of birds, smart investors often follow other smart investors.

However, they may not all arrive at the destination simultaneously or at the same prices, resulting in variations in their positions on the business's value. Some may have paid too little, while others may have paid too much.

When the results of the business value fall short of expectations, many of these capital sources will seek "greener pastures," creating buying opportunities. But as time passes and business algorithms reveal their true nature, perceptions about the solutions they offer will change, and the market will once again appreciate them.

In deciding when to take action, both Charlie Munger and Warren Buffett employ a strategy inspired by baseball superstar and legend Ted Williams. Warren Buffett explains it as follows:

"You don't need to be an expert on every company, or even many companies. You simply need to be able to evaluate companies within your circle of competence. The size of that circle isn't crucial; knowing its boundaries, however, is essential."

Charlie Munger says:

"For the most part, you don't have to do much except find amusement. Occasionally, you'll come across a 'fat pitch'—a slow, straight ball right in your sweet spot. That's when you swing hard."

In the world of investing, exercising smart patience often yields greater rewards than impulsive actions.

According to Warren Buffett, the key is to sit tight and wait until the right opportunity presents itself. Ignore the pressure from others to make a move unless it aligns with your strategy.

But, as Charlie Munger adds, when that golden opportunity arises, you must summon the willpower to give it your all. Take advantage of the favorable odds by utilizing the resources accumulated through past patience and prudence.

My hope is that when you finally encounter the opportunity you've been waiting for, you're prepared to seize it and "get the ball off the field."

Warren Buffett believes that the moment of investment is closely tied to our own capabilities. We don't need to be experts in every industry, but it's crucial to understand the limits of our own competence.

As Buffett points out, unlike in baseball where three strikes result in an out, the most significant penalty in investing is the error of omission—the missed chance to capitalize on an exceptional opportunity.

3.5 Principle of the margin of safety

The Principle of the Margin of Safety teaches us the importance of being humble in recognizing the unpredictable nature of the future, our fallibility as humans, and our limited understanding and ability to act. To ensure the longevity of our investments through uncertain and challenging times, it is wise to take prudent and thoughtful measures.

According to Benjamin Graham, the key to successful investments lies in the concept of the "margin of safety." While nothing is certain, it is far better to be cautious and careful than to chase after excessive wealth.

The margin of safety acts as a protective cushion against errors in our calculations. It means that we should strive to minimize the impact of our ignorance, pride, overconfidence, and inability to predict the future on the capital we allocate.

The more we understand our investments, rely on sound reasoning, and embrace reality, the better equipped we are to avoid situations of poor quality or overpaying for securities of good value.

Charlie Munger reminds us that even a wonderful business does not justify an exorbitant price. It is essential to assess situations where the odds of success are in our favor without the need for undue optimism.

Warren Buffett and Charlie Munger liken the margin of safety to civil engineering design. Just as a bridge designed to support 15 tons only allows trucks weighing five tons to pass, investment decisions should adhere to similar principles.

The complexity of the margin of safety lies in positioning ourselves during abnormal situations where others may misjudge the "subjective value" compared to the "objective value."

The extent of such misjudgment can create a margin of safety, providing room to withstand the risks of human error.

Unlike engineering calculations, establishing safety margins in investments is more challenging due to the complexities of valuations. It requires more than just a correct analysis; there must be a level of confidence that even if mistakes are made, losses can be avoided.

To conduct margin of safety analyses, our primary tool is understanding the fragility of investments in adverse events.

We should only invest in assets that we are willing to hold during economic collapses and that demonstrate the ability to weather crises and emerge stronger from them.

First and foremost, we should avoid ventures that we don't understand technically. Participating in low-quality businesses during favorable conditions exposes us to significant losses.

The best protection against risk is to ensure that algorithms are well-designed and operated by courageous and creative individuals who take action to realize their growth potential.

It is crucial to have compelling evidence that the value of what we purchase far exceeds the price we pay.

3.6 Principle of capital allocation

The Principle of Capital Allocation emphasizes the importance of making intelligent decisions when allocating our capital. We'll exclude those who passively invest in widely diversified mutual funds, as their focus is on minimizing costs and remaining indifferent to market fluctuations.

According to Benjamin Graham, an investment is considered intelligent when it offers relative principal protection and a rational return. This criterion guides us in identifying investment opportunities and acting accordingly.

Our goal is to create a capital structure that safeguards our wealth from the erosion of entropy and the risk of loss. By practicing stewardship, we ensure the betterment of future generations.

To achieve this, we prioritize allocating capital to business algorithms that efficiently solve problems and exhibit consistent growth.

Every investment decision must be made with careful thought, following principles of prudence, rationality, and security. We should understand the specific risks associated with each opportunity, without being swayed by market trends or macroeconomics.

Converting cash into equity generates intrinsic value if done wisely and systematically, rather than relying on guesswork.

We should avoid comparing ourselves to others engaged in similar activities, as each investment portfolio is unique, just as our perspectives and worldviews differ.

In Graham's words, if three individuals with different investment theses were asked to select the "five best American companies" from the S&P 500, it would be nearly impossible for them to generate identical lists.

The perception of whether a security is "expensive" or "cheap" depends largely on one's worldview, expectations, cognitive biases, and personal priorities.

Furthermore, if multiple analysts agree on a business's value, its price will immediately rise, eliminating any advantage or opportunity to acquire it.

What matters is comparing our own performance to the market average, acknowledging our individual capacity to effectively carry out this task. We must recognize our fallibility and limited abilities.

As Benjamin Graham suggests, the more effort we invest in understanding our actions, the greater our profit potential and the more opportunities we will uncover.

Conversely, passivity and a desire for security without concerns will result in lower returns, as we will be participating in opportunities already seized by others.

We disagree with the notion that "the higher the risk, the greater the profit." Taking unnecessary risks does not guarantee better outcomes, just as walking barefoot in a store or on a street does not ensure superior results compared to safer alternatives.

The composition of our portfolio depends on the resources available to us, the future capital we can allocate, and our understanding of our own capabilities.

We should exercise patience when seeking investment prospects that align with our comfort level, similar to how we take time to choose friendships or long-term relationships.

However, we shouldn't hastily divest all our capital, as new opportunities may arise and our knowledge grows through learning and experience.

Applying the compound interest formula, $X_f = X_0 (1 + r)^n$, our goal is to preserve the initial capital and maximize dividend returns. We strive to minimize costs and conduct iterations to achieve greater capital growth.

Rather than excessive diversification, we prefer appropriate concentration.

As Andrew Carnegie said, "We will put all the eggs in one basket, and we will watch the basket." We avoid prospects of poor quality or businesses we don't understand to steer clear of mediocrity.

Our attention is focused on thoroughly understanding prospects that meet our criteria. However, we remain aware that no investment is permanent, as there is a principle of diminishing returns that reminds us that growth has its limits.

When we recognize a mistake, it's best to correct it promptly. Just like the investor in the parable of stewardship, if a portion of our portfolio is in an undesirable situation, we release those funds and allocate them to opportunities that can generate substantial profits.

Mistakes should not be ignored or taken lightly. We shouldn't indulge in self-pity or react with unwarranted anger. Instead, we carefully document our mistakes to learn from errors of omission and commission.

We should be cautious during speculative market seasons. It's unwise to settle for small gains from good investments while holding onto poor ones.

According to Philip Fisher, we should never sell for short-term reasons. Our investment decisions should have a minimum one-year horizon, and we must be prepared to hold investments for more than five years.

However, we should consider divesting when we realize a mistake over time or when fundamental changes occur in the business algorithm's operation.

If the opportunity's potential is nearing exhaustion, if the algorithm's competitive advantage is eroding, or if significantly higher-value opportunities with substantial growth rates emerge, divestment may be advisable.

4 Appendix

Here is a table that presents the principles set out in this work with a brief reminder of their meaning.

Principles of purpose

Reasons and motives for capital allocation

Principle	Brief reminder
Value	Its value is conscience. Value has current capacity for "the good" in our lives. It also improves our present and our future.
Character	It is the only thing we can control. Avoid failures, develop humility, curiosity, and perseverance. Let's conduct ourselves with integrity, ingenuity, and hard work. It is the basis for us and others to enjoy our courageous character.
Entropy	The direction of things in the physical universe is that everything increasingly degrades into chaos and disorder. Therefore, " everything wears out of service " and "trees do not grow to the sky".

Principle	Brief reminder
Problems	They arise from the advancement of life within a world subjected to entropy. Therefore, each solution to a problem generates new problems.
Future	The future is different, inevitable, unpredictable. We will seek positions of protection against damage and act today to tame the future tomorrow.
Capital	It is a technology developed by mankind. It is a system with the capacity to store value. It is the nature of the growth of things. Do not idolize it, put it at your service. Use it to build a better future.
Businesses	They are algorithms with which we refuse leisure to solve social problems. If they are based on capital, their purpose is to spread and endure to solve more and more problems.

Principles of form

Principles to understand the right path for capital allocation

Principle	Brief reminder
Analysis	It serves to describe and criticize the situation and, if it is used to analyze business, then make a business decision. It should be practical, with depth depending on what is at stake. Let it be with care and skepticism. Pay special attention with mental traps and prejudices.
Macroeconomics	It is better to understand the environment where the businesses that interest us interact than to try to anticipate it to try to discover opportunities.
Money inflation	It is the increase in the cost of living. It is inevitable because of entropy. Its rhythm affects the meaning of our daily decisions. Cash is more powerful as a storage of value and a capacity to take advantage of bargains.
Credit interest	It is the general cost of lending money to others and influences the dynamism of business and consumption.

Principle	Brief reminder
Taxes for the public interest	It is necessary to collaborate in the implementation of a political power that meets the needs of the society in which we interact and from which we obtain economic benefits.
Financial system	It is the basis of the perception of economic and political power of a currency. It supports the financing configuration for the operation of business algorithms. It is complex and defines the environment for economic development.
International business	It is based on the differences in comparative position between one society and another. Its configuration is based on geographic position, resources and technological capacity which define the orientation of supply chains.
Industry	We seek to understand the general configuration of the offering that currently solves problems of a kind. The best role models are those of leaders and those who grow above average.
Seeking opportunities	Separation of "the good", the "mediocre" and the "bad". It takes time, dedication, and effort. It demands a courageous character and that there are

Principle	Brief reminder
	favorable situations for the abundance of opportunities.
Business securities	We will seek opportunities in accordance with the three Charlie Munger principles (pun intended): 1. a great business at a fair price is superior to a fair business at a great price 2. a great business at a fair price is superior to a fair business at a great price, 3. a great business at a fair price is superior to a fair business at a great price.
Stewardship	It is the responsibility to care for, nurture, and safeguard the values of others. Its absence in a prospectus rules out any capital allocation interest.
Creativity	It is the essence for a business algorithm to update itself as situations change given entropy, and to keep solving problems and continuously generating new values.
Distribution	Very little value is obtained if a solution to a problem is found, and it is kept from others.

Principles of act

To act and not act in the capital allocation process

Principle	Brief reminder
Investing	According to Benjamin Graham, it is an intelligent act of capital allocation in which there is relative safety of conserving de principal and expecting a rational return. If these three conditions do not exist, we are talking about speculation.
The investment approach	There are two schools and their variants. The first is protection against an uncertain future. This is, to buy cheap and sell expensive. The second is to partner in businesses with a promising future and aggressive growth. Both can create great fortunes thanks to a courageous character and if the proper principles are applied.
The market	The market is extremely intelligent and your opinion will not always be rational. Every day its getting larger and more complex, has more technology and reaches more places.

Principle	Brief reminder
The moment of investment	"Wait for the ball to reach your area of competence." It is always a good moment to enter a quality business with a correct price. It is never a good time to get out of quality business.
Margin of safety	Protection against our calculation errors. For Benjamin Graham, "it is much better to be careful and cautious than to try to make all the money in the world."
Capital allocation	It is based on a courageous character. Let's avoid excuses and learn from our mistakes. It should be done with the greatest possible awareness. We must prefer businesses ran by people who are honest, creative, and that have the ability to extend them as something better into the future, as when we establish long-term friendly relationships.

5 Bibliographic references

1687, England. *Mathematical principles of natural philosophy*, Isaac Newton.

1776, Scotland. *The Wealth of Nations*, Adam Smith.

1867, Germany. *The Capital*, Karl Marx.

1879, England. *The Mechanical theory of heat*, Rudolf Clasius.

1916, Germany. *General Theory of Relativity*, Albert Einstein.

1934, United States. *Security Analysis*, Benjamin Graham and David Dodd.

1946, Germany. *Man's Search for Meaning*, Viktor E. Frankl.

1949, United States. *The Intelligent Investor*, Benjamin Graham.

1958, United States. *Common Stocks and Uncommon Profits and Other Writings*, Philip A. Fisher.

1960, United States. *Paths to Wealth Through Common Stocks*, Philip A. Fisher.

1963, England. *Conjectures and refutations*, Karl Popper.

1976, England. *Surveiller et puni*, Michel Foucault.

2005, United States. *Poor Charlie's Almanac: The Wit and Wisdom of Charles T. Munger*, edited by Peter D. Kaufman.

2006, Mexico. *20 thesis of Politics*, Enrique Dussel.

2008, United States. *The Ascent of Money: A Financial History of the World*, Niall Ferguson.

2014, United States. *Zero to One: Notes on Startups or How to Build the Future*, Peter Thiel.

1965-2018, United States. *Annual Letters to Berkshire Hathaway Shareholders*, Warren E. Buffett.

6 Personal thanks

The year 2019 was complex for me due to the many changes that I experienced on a personal level. I had very pleasant experiences, while some events were extraordinarily painful to me. I honestly do not remember having lived such an adverse year.

In one sentence, the Preacher of Ecclesiastes says that: "In the day of good, enjoy good; and in the day of adversity, consider" and I think this was a year of consideration. This work combines ten years of compilation and study, and after reflection I decided to finish it as a product to share.

During this time I have talked and lived with an innumerable number of people who, sometimes without knowing it, have contributed with points of view that have served as a starting point for thought, so it is impossible for me to name them all.

My specific thanks to a few people who have impacted the way that I see the world, and who in one way or another helped me complete this process, without chronological order or specific frequency.

To my parents Guillermo and Selizeth, for teaching me the value of faith in the Divine and for their love.

To my brothers Karla, David, and Daniel Estefani, for teaching me the value of unconditional family support.

To Carolina Vázquez, for having taught me the value of trust.

To César Arias, for teaching me the value of nobility and friendship.

To Alejandro Carrillo, for teaching me the value of a good food.

To Carlos Guzmán and Oscar Suárez, for teaching me the value of enjoying life on this Earth.

To Jorge Rossano, for teaching me the value of understanding the nature of power.

To Pieter Koopman, for teaching me the value of fellowship and leadership.

To Roxana Zermeño, for her pleasant company as editor and for her observations to perfect the text you just read.

To Hugo Briseño Ramírez, for his magnanimity and for teaching me the value of passion for science. Furthermore, without his invaluable support as editor, this document would never have come close enough to see the light of day.

I also consider that there are people who are important in the development of maturity. They teach us aspects such as trust or remind us of our principles. They teach us from our mistakes, how we should not think, behave, or treat people. I doubt that you will get to know this document, but with joy I express my understanding, empathy, and gratitude. You know who you are.

To the authors of the bibliographic references, who at some point concluded that it was better to teach us something new and good than to keep it for their own benefit, leaving us their thoughts and knowledge in the hope that strangers from the future could improve our lives.

Guadalajara, Jalisco, February 2020.

7 About the author

I studied International Business and a master's degree in Finance at the Universidad Panamericana in Guadalajara, Mexico.

In my professional beginnings I participated in the management for the development of projects for the exploitation of mineral values in the northwest of Mexico. Since I focused on business analysis ten years ago, I design and build private investment portfolios in Mexico following these principles.

I am currently Chairman of the Board and Chief Executive Officer of the company Bina Ormasel, S.A.P.I. de C.V.

www.ingramcontent.com/pod-product-compliance
Lightning Source LLC
Chambersburg PA
CBHW060836220526
45466CB00003B/1129